Improve your aural!

Paul Harris and John Lenehan

Contents

fabermusic.com

© 2006 by Faber Music Ltd
First published in 2006 by Faber Music Ltd
Updated edition first published in 2010
Bloomsbury House 74–77 Great Russell Street London WC1B 3DA
Music processed by Music Set 2000
Design by Susan Clarke
Printed in England by Caligraving Ltd
All rights reserved

ISBN10: 0-571-53546-1
EAN13: 978-0-571-53546-0

CD recorded in Rectory Studio, High Wycombe, April 2006
Created and produced by John Lenehan
Thanks to Godstowe School Chamber Choir 2006
Track 35 Excerpt from 'Song of the Black Swan' performed by Lowri Blake (cello) and Hugh Webb (harp). Used by kind permission of the performers. www.lowrirecords.com
Track 36 ℗ and © 1988–2006, licensed by kind permission of Naxos Rights International Ltd
All other tracks
℗ 2006 Faber Music Ltd
© 2006 Faber Music Ltd

Why is aural important?

You may wonder why you have to do aural at all. The answer is, that aural will really help you improve as a musician. And this may surprise you – it will help perhaps more than *any other* single musical skill.

Aural is all about understanding and processing music that you hear and see, in your head. By doing so, you will find that your own playing improves enormously. You will be able to play more expressively and stylistically, be more sensitive to quality and control of tone, your music reading will improve, you will be able to spot your own mistakes, be more sensitive to others when playing or singing in an ensemble, be more aware of intonation, improve your ability to memorise music and improve your ability to improvise and compose.

All the many elements of musical training are of course connected. So, when working through the activities in this book you will be connecting with many of them. You'll be listening, singing, clapping, playing your instrument, writing music down, improvising and composing – as well as developing that vital ability to do well at the aural tests in your grade exams!

Aural is not an occasional optional extra – just to be taken off a dusty shelf a few days (or even hours) before a music exam. It's something you can be developing and thinking about all the time. And as you go through the enjoyable and fun activities in these books you'll realise how important and useful having a good musical ear (being good at aural) really is.

How to use this book

When you have a few minutes to spare (perhaps at the beginning or end of a practice session), sit down with your instrument, by your CD player, and open this book. Choose a section and then work through the activities – you needn't do much each time. But whatever you do, do it carefully, repeating any activity if you feel it will help. In fact many of the activities will be fun to do again and again. And make sure that you come back to the book on a regular basis.

So, good luck and enjoy improving your aural skills!

Paul Harris and John Lenehan

For U.S. readers:
Bar = Measure
Note = Tone
Tone = Whole Step

Section 1 Clapping rhythms

 Listen to this track – you don't have to remember this piece. Instead just be aware of any melodic or rhythmic patterns in the music. When we listen to speech we absorb both the general meaning and groups of words or phrases – rarely do we focus on one individual word. Similarly in music there are usually patterns to hear which makes remembering longer rhythms or melodies much easier. When we try to remember a longer rhythm or melody we might be trying *too hard*. Simply listen and absorb. Stay focused, think forwards, and don't allow any of the following (or similar) thoughts to slip into your consciousness:

'This is too long'

'I can't remember the opening bit'

'I can't do this'

Simply remain cool, calm and collected!

listening activities

 1 Now, in a state of complete calmness, listen to each of these rhythms. Clap them back straight away. Don't think about them!

2 Here are some more rhythms to clap back. After you've clapped each rhythm, write down whether it was in 2, 3 or 4-time.

 3 After you've heard each phrase on this track, improvise your own rhythmic answer. The first one is done for you as an example. Use elements from the given phrase in your response.

4 Using a piece you are currently learning, clap or tap the rhythm of the whole piece with your right hand (on a table for example) and the pulse with your left hand. Now repeat, swapping hands. Now tap the pulse with your right foot and clap or tap the rhythm.

5 Now try to hear the first four bars in your head, and then, without looking at the music, have a go at answering the following questions:

- How many beats are there in each bar? _____

- Does the piece have an up-beat? _____

- Is it in simple or compound time? _____

- Are there any rests in the first four bars? _____

- Write down the rhythm of the melody of the first four bars. Put in the time signature:

Come back and repeat this exercise using other pieces or using other four-bar phrases from the same piece.

listening activities

1 Listen to the following phrases, each of which you'll hear three times. Play the tracks again if you need to. Then write each down (both the rhythm and the melody).

2 Now sing the melodies from the notation, and then play them on your instrument. Then, in your head, hear the melodies backwards. Do you recognize the tunes? You'll find the answers on p.16.

3 On these six tracks you'll hear tunes for you to repeat. Each one is played twice. You may like to try playing them on your instrument as well. These are the starting notes for each track:

Track 12: C

Track 13: A

Track 14: E♭

Track 15: A

Track 16: C

Track 17: G

5

Singing from notation

listening activities

1 In Grade 5 you will have to sing six notes in a row. Listen to the following six-note groups which will be played twice, and then write each one down. The first one is done for you.

Now sing each example from the notation and finally play each on your instrument.

2 Here are six patterns for you to sing. Play the first note on your instrument, then hear the pattern in your head. (Notice that each begins and ends on the tonic note.) Sing the pattern and then play it on your instrument.

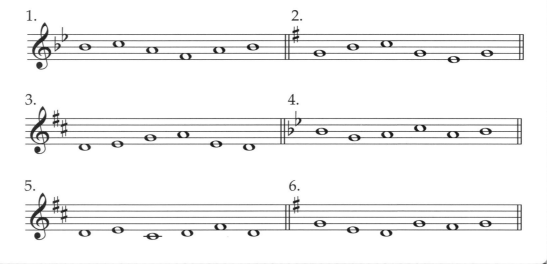

3 On this track there are six more six-note patterns. Follow the music below. One note in each group has been changed. Tick the note that is different.

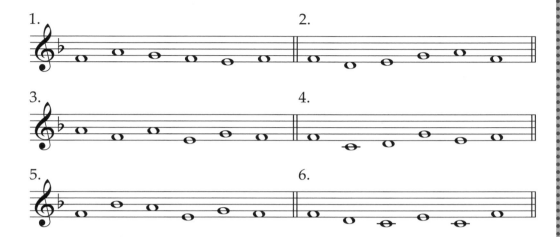

Now sing each example as written.

4 Here are six more patterns for you to sing. Play the first note, then hear the pattern in your head and finally sing the pattern out loud.

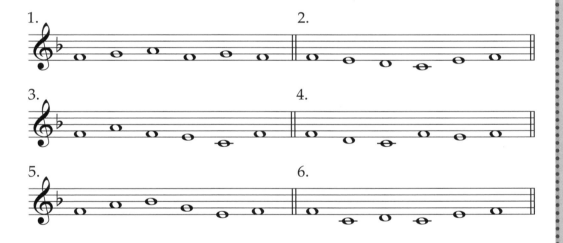

5 Now sing the above patterns using the rhythm ♩ ♩ ♩ | ♩ ♩ ♩ | with the backing track. You'll hear the correct phrase repeated by a saxophone.

Learning to listen to music

In this grade you will be asked about:

- Dynamic levels (varying levels of volume and changes between them)
- Articulation (legato and varying forms of staccato or detached notes)
- Tonality (major or minor)
- Tempo (speed and changes of speed)
- Character
- Style and period

The new feature to learn to listen to and understand is identifying the *style and period* of a piece of music. If you listen intelligently to a wide range of music you will inevitably improve your powers of deduction with time (and the previous *Improve your aural!* books have already introduced this feature).

Here are some useful features to help you identify the four main musical periods:

Baroque

- Use of ornaments
- Two or more independent melodic lines (also known as contrapuntal writing)
- Use of imitation between the parts
- Limited dynamic range or use of 'terraced' dynamics, which means a sudden change from loud to soft, with no crescendo or decrescendo

Classical

- Regular (often four-bar) phrase-lengths
- Use of tune and accompaniment texture (often with arpeggio-like patterns in the accompaniment)
- Symmetrical structure
- Often including simple scale and arpeggio melodic patterns
- Often uses predominantly tonic/dominant harmony

Romantic

- Expressive and vivid use of dynamic levels and other expression markings
- More intricate melodic patterns
- Colourful harmonies
- May be atmospheric, moody or virtuosic in character and style.
- Thicker and more varied textures (for example thicker chords contrasted with single musical lines)

20th/21st century

- Less reliance on major and minor keys
- More complex rhythms
- More extreme ranges of pitch
- Can be dissonant and jazzy. Anything goes!

The secret of success here is to identify at least *two features* when listening to a piece or extract. Just one feature may point you in the wrong direction. For example, though ornaments are a strong feature of the Baroque period, they also occur in the Classical style. But if you hear ornaments in a piece with a limited range of dynamics (or 'terraced' dynamics) and perhaps some imitation between the parts as well, then you can be fairly sure that it *is* Baroque!

Texture

Though 'texture' is not a feature you will be asked about until Grade 6 it can be useful in helping to identify and talk about style. In music, texture describes the parts (or lines or voices) in a piece of music and, where there is more than one part, the relationship between them. In a piano piece, for example, texture could be *thin* – just a single line of music, or *thick* – big chords in each hand, each with four or more notes.

So you might hear any of the following textures:

- A single line of music
- Two or more independent lines played at the same time
- A tune with accompaniment
- Chordal writing

Some pieces (or sections of pieces) might consistently use one form of musical texture throughout. On this track, listen to the examples and connect the correct pairings.

single line texture	played 1st
two independent lines of music	played 2nd
tune and accompaniment	played 3rd
chordal	played 4th

Baroque music will often be written using two (or sometimes more) independent lines of music. The 'tune and accompaniment' texture is often a feature of Classical style music, whilst thicker chords may be more common in Romantic or 20th/21st century music. But don't forget to look for at least two features before you decide on your answers.

Here are some examples to help you identify particular features in music. Listen to the music and pick out the distinctive features:

1 _____

2 _____

3 _____

4 _____

Listen to the pieces on this track and write down which style and period you think each piece comes from. Then list two features which lead you to this answer.

1 _____

_____

2 _____

_____

3 _____

_____

4 _____

_____

5 _____

_____

6 _____

_____

7 _____

_____

8 _____

_____

listening activities

The pieces on the next six tracks combine all the features you might be asked about. Each one will only be played once and then you'll be asked to answer two questions from the following:

1 Describe two features that will help you to identify the style and period.

2 Was it major or minor? Did it change anywhere?

3 What did you notice about the dynamic levels?

4 Is this piece in Baroque, Classical or Romantic style? Why?

5 How does the articulation change throughout the piece?

6 Were there any tempo changes?

7 How would you describe the articulation at the start?

8 How would you describe the character of the music?

track (29)   1 _____

           7 _____

track (30)   6 _____

           8 _____

track (31)   5 _____

           4 _____

track (32)   1 _____

           2 _____

track (33)   3 _____

           4 _____

track (34)   5 _____

           8 _____

2 Using a piece you are currently working on, answer the following:

● How would you best describe the character of the music? Why?

_____

_____

● In which period was the piece written?
Write down two reasons for your answer.

_____

_____

● Is the piece in a major or minor key?

_____

● How do the dynamic markings help to bring character to the music?

_____

● Play the piece really exaggerating all the markings!

● Play the piece reversing all the markings (e.g. p = f, cresc. = dim.,
rall. = accel., etc.)

● Play the piece as expressively as possible, making the most of all the
markings.

Section 5 # Making connections

These fun activities show you how aural connects with all the other aspects of music. Choose one or two each time you practise.

... with instruments

Each of the following four examples are duets. Write down which instruments are playing in each duet.

1 _____

2 _____

3 _____

4 _____

On this track you'll hear two trios. Which instruments are playing in each one?

1 _____

2 _____

... with transposition

Play the first four bars of *Twinkle, twinkle, little star* in C major. Now play the same phrase in F, G, D and B♭ majors.

Now make up your own four-bar phrase in C major. Transpose it (by ear) to the keys of F, G, D and B♭ majors.

... with improvisation

On this track you'll hear a cheerful and lively piece. After each two-bar phrase, improvise your own response. The key is F major – just use the notes: F G A C D (For B♭ instruments, improvise in G major using the notes: G A B D E. E♭ instruments improvise in D major, using the notes: D E F♯ A B.)

... with sight-reading

Choose a sight-reading piece* and try to hear it first in your head. Then play it.

... with intervals

Play a note and then, in your head, hear the note a perfect fifth above (e.g. play C and then hear G). Sing the note and then play it to see how accurate you were. Can you find any perfect fifths in the pieces you are currently studying?

... with markings

Listen to this track as many times as you like. As you hear them, add the dynamics, articulation and tempo indications to the piece, which is written out for you below. Each line begins with a new dynamic level.

There are at least one each of the following:

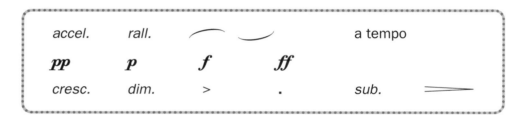

*From *Improve your sight-reading!* Grade 5, for example

14

... with expression

Choose a phrase from a piece that you are currently learning. Now hear it in your head as expressively as possible. Now play the phrase as you heard it in your head.

A final message from the authors!

Style 1 _____

Style 2 _____

Style 3 _____

Answers
(by CD track number)

Section 1: *Clapping rhythms*
4 3   **5** 2   **6** 4   **7** 2   **8** 3

Section 2: *Pitch*
10 Twinkle, twinkle, little star
11 Away in a manger

18 and 19

20 and 21

22 and 23

Section 3: *Singing from notation*
24 1: The 4th note was changed
2: The 4th note was changed
3: The 3rd note was changed
4: The 5th note was changed
5: The 6th note was changed
6: The 2nd note was changed

Section 4: *Learning to listen to music*
26 1st – two independent lines of music
2nd – chordal, 3rd – tune and accompaniment,
4th – single line texture.

27 1: Independent melodic lines, and imitation
between parts.
2: Tonic/dominant harmony, tune with
accompaniment, regular phrase lengths.
3: Atmospheric, colourful harmony and expressive
dynamics.
4: Imitation between parts, some use of
independent melodic lines.

28 1: Baroque (ornaments, independent melodic
lines, imitation)
2: Classical (tune and accompaniment, scale
passages, regular phrase lengths, tonic/dominant
harmony)
3: Romantic (thicker texture, expressive and
colourful harmony)
4: Baroque (ornaments, two independent melodic
lines)
5: Romantic (thicker texture, dramatic dynamics,
colourful harmony, virtuosic)
6: 20/21st Century (extreme pitch range,
dissonance, complexity of rhythm and harmony)

7: Classical (tune and accompaniment, scale
passages, tonic/dominant harmony, regular
phrase lengths)
8: 20/21st Century (dissonant and jazzy feel,
extreme pitch range, complexity of rhythm)

29 1: Regular phrase lengths, use of scale and
arpeggio passages.
2: There was detached (staccato) playing at the
beginning.

30 6: It slowed down at the end.
8: Cheerful, playful, cheeky (at the end).

31 5: Staccato chords at the start, becoming legato.
4: Romantic: stormy character and thick textures.

32 1: Thicker texture, virtuosic, colourful harmonies,
expressive dynamics.
2: Minor (no change)

33 3: There was a quiet section midway through and
then it gradually got louder to the end.
4: Baroque: two independent lines, ornaments.

34 5: Starts very staccato, short legato passage in
the middle, ends quite staccato again.
8: Hesitant, confused, then confident and brash.

Section 5: *Making connections*
35 1: Recorder and glockenspiel
2: Bassoon and harpsichord
3: Cello and harp
4: Clarinet and piano

36 1: Three oboes (or two oboes and a cor anglais)
2: Piano, violin and cello (this combination is
usually called a Piano Trio even though there is
only one piano!)

38

39 1: Classical   2: Baroque   3: Romantic